KEEPSAKE CRAFTS
BEADS

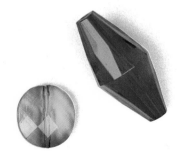

Keepsake Crafts

BEADS

Jo Moody

B.T. Batsford Ltd • London

First published in Great Britain by
B.T. Batsford Ltd.
4 Fitzhardinge Street
London W1H 0AH

Copyright © 1994 Quarto Publishing plc

A QUARTO BOOK

ISBN 0-7134-7608-7

A catalogue record for this book is available from the British Library.

This book was designed and produced by
Quarto Publishing plc
The Old Brewery
6 Blundell Street
London N7 9BH

Senior editor Sally MacEachern
Editors Geraldine Christy, Jane Royston
Senior art editor Amanda Bakhtiar
Designer Allan Mole
Photographers Paul Forrester, Chas Wilder
Illustrator Elsa Godfrey
Art director Moira Clinch
Editorial director Sophie Collins

Typeset by Poole Typesetting, Bournemouth
Manufactured in Hong Kong by
Regent Publishing Services Ltd
Printed in China by Leefung-Asco
Printers Ltd

CONTENTS

INTRODUCTION   6

MATERIALS   8

TECHNIQUES   10

MAKING YOUR OWN BEADS   14

WRAPPED IN GOLD   16

JAZZY JEANS JACKET   18

TOP CLASS   20

VESTED INTERESTS   22

EVENING SHIMMER   24

STARRY NIGHTS   26

JET SET   28

BEDAZZLING BAG   30

JEWEL BRIGHT   32

SENSATIONAL SEASONINGS   52

LIGHT SHOW   54

WINDOW DRESSING   56

TREE TREASURES   58

BOLD BANDS   34

BELTING UP   36

HEAD TURNERS   38

GLAMOROUS GLOVES   40

TASSELS & TIEBACKS   42

CHARMING COVERS   44

MADE WITH LOVE   46

FESTIVE BAUBLES   60

CHIMERICAL CHIMES   62

ACKNOWLEDGMENTS   64

FLORAL FANTASY   48

CRYSTAL & CANDLELIGHT   50

INTRODUCTION

Beads have featured in jewellery design and decorative art for well over five thousand years, and have always been highly prized. They have been worn as symbols to display both power and wealth, traded for gold, ivory and even slaves, and in some cultures used to ward off evil. The history of beads has often mirrored social, economic and even political events through the centuries, and is certainly worth studying if you have the chance.

Beads are available today in a wonderful array of shapes and sizes, and come in such a kaleidoscopic range of colours, with transparent, opaque, metallic, iridescent and natural finishes, that they are one of the most exciting materials with which to work. The major bead "types" are shown here.

GLASS BEADS

Tiny glass beads, often used in decorative embroidery, are known as rocailles or seed beads. Tube-shaped bugle beads are perfect for embroidery and bead fringes. Larger coloured-glass beads are ideal for jewellery, and, if faceted, reflect the light superbly, making them ideal for tassels and fringes.

PLASTIC BEADS

Plastic beads can be moulded and faceted to resemble glass, and are much lighter and less expensive than the real thing. They can also have a metallic finish.

WOODEN BEADS

Wooden beads give a natural feel to clothing and jewellery. They may be plain, highly polished to show off the natural grain, carved, or painted with bright primary colours.

METAL BEADS

Metal beads with gold, silver or bronze finishes are very useful. They range from bright, shiny, modern beads in irregular shapes to beautiful antique-style beads with inset decoration. Metal beads create rich effects for jewellery or accessories.

CERAMIC BEADS

Ceramic beads, made from fired clay, are often exquisitely decorated and are perfect for colourful jewellery. Synthetic clays can also be used to give a similar effect. Stone beads often have a beautiful glazed finish.

EMBROIDERY STONES

Flat-backed "jewel" beads are ideal for use on practical items such as bags or cushions, as they will not catch on other objects. They usually have small holes on either side for attaching to fabric, but can also have a single central hole.

NATURAL BEADS

Carved or smooth bone beads have a lovely texture and look wonderful on clothing and for chunky jewellery. Plastic imitations are available if you prefer, and make a cheaper alternative. The iridescent quality of synthetic-pearl beads makes a beautiful decoration on almost any surface.

SEQUINS

Although not technically beads, bright metallic and iridescent sequins are often used alongside beads to add detail and texture.

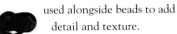

NOVELTY BEADS

Colourful novelty beads make fun pieces of jewellery or decoration on children's clothes or accessories.

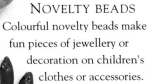

MATERIALS

Most of the projects in this book require very little in the way of specialist materials and equipment, although there are a few basic items that you will need. You may well already have these in your sewing or household tool box, but, if not, they are inexpensive to buy and readily available from the local shopping centre, from specialist craft outlets and by mail order.

Having the correct equipment at hand will make working the projects much easier and will also give a professional finish, so it is worth investing in the right tools before you start. Shown here are the basic items you will need.

PLIERS

Small jeweller's pliers with fine, smooth tips are needed for shaping jewellery findings. If these do not have a cutting edge, wire-cutters will also be needed.

FINDINGS

Findings are the metal components used for jewellery, and are usually made from a base metal plated with a silver, gold or nickel solution.

1 Jump rings link various jewellery components and findings. **2** Triangle bails are used to hang thicker beads, which will not take a jump ring. **3** Eye pins are threaded through beads to link them together and to other findings. **4** Head pins are used in the same way as eye pins.

5 Screw clasps consist of two halves which screw together. **6** Pierced-ear wires come in various shapes. **7** Bell caps conceal multi-strand thread ends on a necklace or earrings. **8** Brooch backs provide a base for sewn or glued beads. **9** Posts with butterfly fastenings for pierced ears. **10** Decorative clasps secure the ends of necklaces and bracelets. **11** Screw and clip fastenings for non-pierced ears.

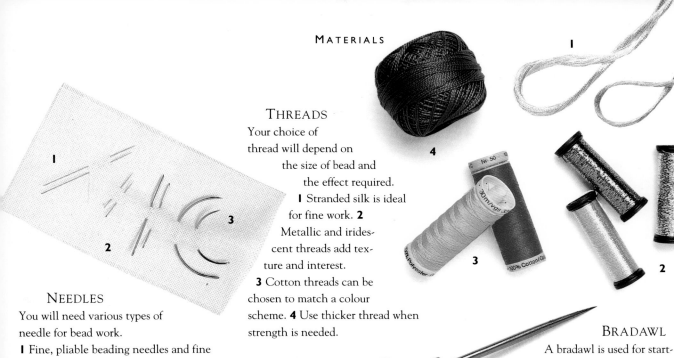

THREADS

Your choice of thread will depend on the size of bead and the effect required. **1** Stranded silk is ideal for fine work. **2** Metallic and iridescent threads add texture and interest. **3** Cotton threads can be chosen to match a colour scheme. **4** Use thicker thread when strength is needed.

NEEDLES

You will need various types of needle for bead work.
1 Fine, pliable beading needles and fine quilting needles are both extremely useful.
2 Leather needles are strong with sharp, angled points. **3** Curved needles are invaluable for stitching beads to awkward shapes.

BRADAWL

A bradawl is used for starting a hole in leather or hide prior to stitching on beads with a needle.

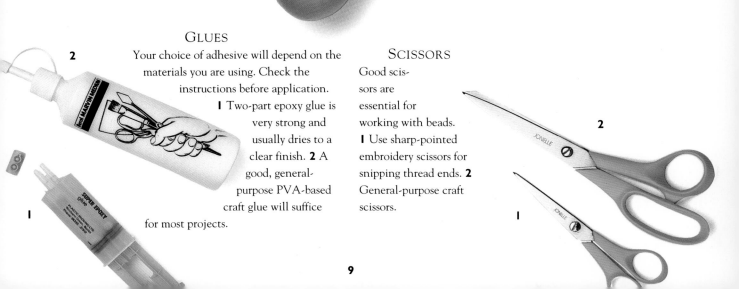

GLUES

Your choice of adhesive will depend on the materials you are using. Check the instructions before application.
1 Two-part epoxy glue is very strong and usually dries to a clear finish. **2** A good, general-purpose PVA-based craft glue will suffice for most projects.

SCISSORS

Good scissors are essential for working with beads.
1 Use sharp-pointed embroidery scissors for snipping thread ends. **2** General-purpose craft scissors.

TECHNIQUES

Each of the projects in this book has its own set of instructions, but there are some basic techniques for working with beads that are useful to know. These will enable you to add a professional finish to your work, and will make the difference between items that feel "home-made" and pieces of work that look expensive and shop-bought.

HOW TO WORK KNOTS

Knotting between the beads gives an authentic Victorian look to necklaces and bracelets, and using a colourful silk or textured thread will also enhance the look of the beads. It is important that the knots you make are large enough not to slip into the bead holes, so use several strands of thread if necessary.

A basic knot will be adequate for most purposes. For a knotted necklace or bracelet, begin with a knot, thread on a bead and loosely form the next knot, using a needle to draw it up close to the bead. Continue in this way, making the knots as even as possible, finish with a knot and work the thread ends back through the beads to conceal them. Add a finding to each end to complete the necklace or bracelet.

If you require a more secure knot, take the thread through the loop of the knot twice, and use a needle to pull it up close to a bead or finding.

A figure-of-eight knot gives a solid finish and is useful when securing thread ends inside a calotte (see page 13).

EMBROIDERING BEADS INDIVIDUALLY

Applying a lot of beads individually to fabric requires patience, but is well worth the effort. Fabric is the easiest surface for this, but you can also apply beads to leather with the help of a bradawl (see page 9).

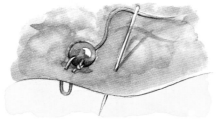

For rocailles, seed beads and round beads, use a fine beading needle and either matching or invisible thread. Tie a knot in one end of the thread, take the needle through from the right side and make two or three tiny stitches on the wrong side (the knot will be concealed by the first bead). Take the needle through to the right side again and thread on the first bead, bringing the needle back through to the wrong side close to the end of the bead, so that it lies firmly in place.

Make a back stitch every third bead or so to give the work a secure finish.

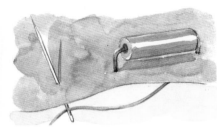

To sew bugle beads, fasten the thread as before and thread on the first bugle. With the bead lying flat on the fabric, take the needle back through to the wrong side close to the edge of the bead, and bring it up again a bugle bead's width away. Apply the next bead by taking the thread from right to left through the bead as if you were making a back stitch, and continue in the same way.

Couching beads

An alternative method of attaching beads is to thread them to make a string, which is then couched to the fabric.

Cut two lengths of invisible or matching thread. Make a knot in the end of one thread, bring it through to the surface of the fabric and thread on the beads. With another needle and the second thread, make a neat overcast stitch as closely as possible to the first bead on the string. Slide the next bead up to it and make the next stitch, and so on, following your design. To complete, finish off the couching thread neatly on the wrong side of the fabric, followed by the strung thread.

Bead fringes

Decorative fringes can be created using various methods, of which the most common is to apply individually beaded strands. These can be worked in two ways.

Decide on the length required for the strands, and cut each thread to twice this length, plus a little extra to allow for sewing the finished strands in place. Thread on the beads, taking one end of the thread through the bottom bead and then both ends of the thread back up through the rest of the beads. Oversew each strand to the fabric or braid as required.

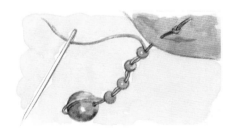

Alternatively, fasten a long thread to the fabric (see "Embroidering Beads Individually"). Thread on enough beads to make a drop of the right length. Take

the thread around the bottom bead and then back up to the top through all the other beads. Bring the thread through to the wrong side and back down again a small stitch further along the fabric. Repeat to make the next strand.

A looped fringe also makes an attractive decoration. Fasten a long thread to the fabric (see "Embroidering Beads Individually" on page 10), and thread on enough beads to create a loop of the desired drop. Take the thread through to the wrong side in the same place, and back down again a small stitch further along.

BEAD TASSELS

Beaded tassels can look extremely effective on jewellery, soft furnishings and even clothes, and are simple to make.

Decide on the number and length of strands you require, and cut this number of threads to twice this length plus enough to allow for taking through a large bead at the top, knotting and securing to fabric. For each strand, thread on the beads, take one end of the thread through the bottom bead, then both ends back up through the rest of the beads. Complete all the strands in this way, and then take all the thread ends through a single large bead and make a secure knot. Oversew the tassel to fabric or attach it to jewellery as required.

USING FINDINGS

These metal components have a wide range of uses in jewellery making.

Head and eye pins are pre-formed lengths of soft wire, and are useful for making basic earrings. Thread on beads to the desired length, trim away any excess pin with wire-cutters, and then use pliers to turn a loop at the top end. This loop can then be joined to an ear wire.

Two or more beaded head or eye pins can be linked to make earrings, as well as bracelets and necklaces.

Large beads can be turned into pendant earrings and necklaces using a triangle bail, which is simply opened out with pliers, inserted into the bead holes and then squeezed into shape to secure.

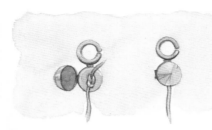

Calottes are particularly useful when making bracelets or necklaces. They are used to conceal knots and join the thread to a jump ring, or directly to a clasp.

Bell caps can also be used to conceal knots at each end of a bracelet or necklace. Knot the threads on to an eye pin and push this through the central hole of the bell cap. Trim the pin to fit, and turn a loop in the end with pliers. You can then link this to a jump ring or directly to a clasp.

BEAD WEAVING

Beads can be woven to create the most decorative pieces in wonderful colour combinations. Experiment with different designs, and work out your pattern beforehand using coloured crayons on plain paper.

A basic bead-lace braid is an ideal first project. The thread follows a regular pattern of loops worked in a zigzag pattern to form the honeycomb effect. Begin working as many loops as necessary to create the desired width, taking the thread back through a bead (shaded in the illustration) in the previous row each time.

Follow the same method to work a wider piece, again taking the thread back through a bead in each previous row.

When the piece reaches the required size, strengthen the weaving by running an additional thread through the beads at the outer edge.

To make the fastening, knot a new thread to one end of the weaving and work a simple loop, as shown, knotting the thread end and working it back in to conceal it. Knot a new thread to the opposite end and thread on some small beads, as shown. Next, take the thread through a medium-sized bead, through a large bead, and then back through the medium-sized bead. Thread on a few more small beads to complete the loop, and finish off the thread with a knot.

MAKING YOUR OWN BEADS

Making your own beads is easy and fun. Papier mâché can be used to create light-weight beads of any size for decoration with your own designs. Marbled beads are also simple to make from Fimo or similar modelling material, as are millefiori beads, based on Venetian glass-making techniques. Pressed-cotton balls also make good bases for colourful decoration.

PAPIER-MACHÉ BEADS

2 When completely dry, slice the ball in half using a craft knife and remove the Plasticine. Glue the paper shell back together, smoothing over any rough edges with another layer or two of papier mâché.

When this is dry, brush over the bead with white paint to cover the newsprint, before painting the ball with your design.

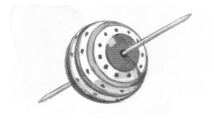

3 When the paint is dry, pierce the bead with a needle to make holes for stringing.

MARBLED BEADS

1 Knead two or three colours of Fimo modelling clay until soft and roll them into sausage shapes. Twist the sausages together. Continue to knead and twist the colours together until you achieve the marbled effect. Do not over-knead the clay, or you will lose the effect.

2 Roll out the marbled clay evenly and cut it into slices using a sharp craft knife. Roll into balls.

1 Roll a piece of Plasticine into a ball. Cut some newspaper into small strips, paint the strips with PVA adhesive or wallpaper paste, and allow this to soak in well before covering the ball with several layers.

3 Push the beads on to cocktail sticks or wooden skewers and bake them in the oven, following the maker's instructions.

4 Paint or spray a light, even coat of varnish over the beads. Leave them to dry thoroughly. String the beads to make the jewellery or decoration of your choice.

MILLEFIORI BEADS

1 To make the design shown here, take Fimo modelling clay in dark blue, green,

mid-blue, red and yellow (or the colours of your choice), and knead them until soft. Roll out thin pieces of dark blue and green clay, place them together and then roll them up to make a spiral design. Roll out a sausage shape of red, and roll a thin layer of mid-blue evenly around it. Cut the sausage shape into several lengths.

2 Make similar lengths of yellow clay, and, alternating this with the blue-and-red roll, stick them around the spiral as shown. Reroll the clay gently to maintain the shape.

3 Roll out a thin piece of dark blue clay, and roll this around the inner colours, keeping it as even as possible. Roll out the finished sausage more thinly.

4 Cut the sausage into slices with a sharp craft knife. Use the slices to make the designs of your choice, by sticking them around a clay base as shown. Form the central holes with a pointed stick, and bake in the oven. Thread the beads on to findings to make colourful earrings, bracelets and necklaces.

PRESSED-COTTON BALLS

Pressed-cotton balls are ideal for bead making. Simply pierce your chosen balls with a needle, and then decorate them in any manner you choose. Use bright or metallic paint colours on their own, or as a base on which to add sequins or rocailles. Paint or spray the finished balls with varnish to complete.

Bead embroidery can become a totally absorbing hobby

which amply rewards the little time and patience that it

requires. This beautiful stole is simple to work and needs

no special skills — just those of basic needlecraft. The floral

WRAPPED IN GOLD

pattern provides a perfect

ready-made template, and

the beads simply follow the outline, so there is no

complicated working out of a design to do.

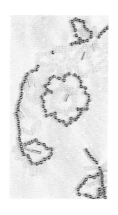

To make a stole for yourself, first choose a suitable fabric. I have used a heavy satin with a subtle, self-coloured pattern, which is ideal for evening wear. It is worth searching through remnant boxes, especially those of the bridal and evening-dress fabric departments in stores, for rich, sumptuous materials. Embroider the fabric with the design of your choice, then line it and sew co-ordinating tassels into each of the corners.

To start the bead decoration, begin by pressing the fabric and laying it out on a flat surface. Examine the pattern carefully to see how it falls. Plan the way that you wish the finished stole to look, and decide whether to bead the outlines of each motif, every other motif or just to work a border design. Next, cut off a small piece of fabric and work a test motif to check the design. This will also enable you to estimate the number of beads you will need.

Always secure the beads to the fabric invisibly. There are several ways of applying them: the most common methods involve either sewing on each bead individually, or using couching to secure a string of beads. For the best results, use a fine thread and a beading needle fine enough to slip through even the tiniest rocaille. Details of these embroidery techniques can be found on pages 10–11.

Tiny gold and pearl

beads cleverly

highlight the pattern

on this cream satin

to make an elegant

evening stole.

JAZZY JEANS JACKET

The customizing of basic jeans jackets is a favourite pastime of top designers. Giving an item of clothing your own individual stamp is easy, and you can be confident that no one else will have the same style in their wardrobe.

An everyday denim jacket is transformed into a real original (opposite) by using beads to embroider motifs and form decorative fringing. A detail of the beading is shown above.

You could decorate the jacket all over, or just highlight certain details, as in the example shown. Here, bead outlines follow top-stitching detail, and the lower edge has also been given a fringed finish similar to a cowboy-style jacket. Motifs in the shapes of hearts and kisses have been embroidered in between.

To highlight the top stitching, string beads on to invisible thread and then couch them in place (see page 11), still using invisible thread. Draw the motifs on the fabric freehand with tailor's chalk, and then stitch the beads in place, following the outlines.

For the perfect finishing touch, add a loop-and-tassel fringe along the lower edge

of the design. To work this, secure a long length of invisible thread on the wrong side of the fabric at one end and bring the needle through to the right side, immediately below a bead highlighting the top stitching. For the tassels, thread nine beads on to the thread, then take the needle back up through all but the bottom bead so that it holds the string. Take the needle back through to the wrong side and up again two or three beads further along. For the loops, thread on the beads (ten in this case), and take the needle through to the wrong side to form a loop. Continue in the same way across the jacket.

Over-the-top decoration with brightly coloured "jewels" works beautifully on this simple camisole.

TOP CLASS

Bold and bedazzling, there is nothing understated about this eye-catching top. The rich jewel colours embroidered on to sophisticated cream satin create a sizzling effect that is just right for the party season.

Lay out the camisole on a flat surface and place the beads on top, working out your design before stitching them in position. You could choose a simple design of small stones to emphasize the cut cleverly, or be more outrageous and cover the piece entirely. Create a bright and jazzy top by using lots of colours together, as shown here, or achieve a softer effect with one or two colours in less vibrant shades.

The flat-backed stones have a hole on either side, just above the base, and are easy to sew on. Using a fine invisible thread and a beading needle, bring the thread up from the wrong side, take it through the holes in the stone and back through to the wrong side, pulling the thread firmly to keep the stone in place. Take care not to catch or pucker the fabric, as this will spoil the appearance of the garment. Bring the thread back up, close to the next stone, and continue working in the same way. Depending on the type of fabric and the ornateness of your design, you may find it easier to apply a lightweight iron-on interfacing to the wrong side of the fabric to give a firmer backing and to prevent the weight of the beads from dragging it down.

A unique beaded cap, finished with a trim of tiny beads on the lower edge and a copper spiral on the top.

A basic waistcoat makes an excellent foil for any form of decoration, from fabric painting to exquisite embroidery. Here, beautiful fabrics and an eclectic mix of tiny beads, sequins, found objects and embroidery materials have been combined to produce a unique piece of clothing.

VESTED INTERESTS

The secret of the beauty of this cap and waistcoat is the intricate detail on the fabric, which is simple to re-create by anyone with basic needle skills, a little imagination and plenty of patience.

Use a rich, heavy brocade for the front fabric, and top this with a layer of fine net. Cover this densely with tiny sequins and glass rocailles, and metalwork embroidery threads. Add interest by using small fluted and filigree bell caps secured with tiny beads and miniature ribbon rosettes to highlight larger beads.

This spectacular waistcoat is covered lavishly with tiny sequins, glass rocailles, bell caps, ribbon rosettes, swirls of copper and metalwork embroidery threads.

Work the main embroidery before making up and lining the waistcoat. Oversew the edges to prevent fraying while you work, and remember not to work too close to buttonholes, or to seams if you plan to machine stitch the pieces together or to add a rich corded edge. You can add detail to these areas after making up the waistcoat, taking care to stitch through the top layer of fabric only.

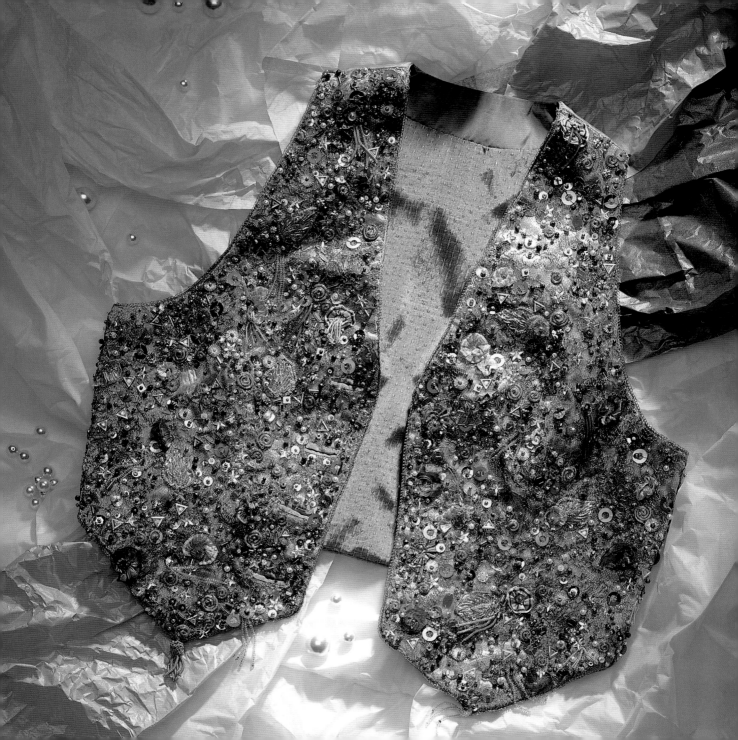

A classic shirt dressed up with subtle beadwork

becomes a beautiful original. Worn with a watch

which has a strap woven from co-ordinating

beads, the effect is a dazzling duo for evenings out.

Highlighting the stitching with

bugle beads, and "spotting" the body with

tiny rocailles, gives this dark-coloured shirt

an understated elegance.

EVENING SHIMMER

The rocailles on the shirt opposite were sewn on individually using a fine beading needle and a single strand of silk embroidery thread, and matching bugles were added to complete the shimmering effect.

You could create a more complex look by covering the collar, cuffs and pocket tops completely with an elaborate embroidered design.

The delicate effect on the watch strap is achieved by hand weaving. Fold two long lengths of nylon thread in half and attach to the bar on one

side of the watch. Thread a gold rocaille on to each double thread. Thread a bugle bead on to just one of the double threads, and push the other double thread through the bugle in the opposite direction, so that the threads cross inside the bead and it lies horizontally instead of vertically.

Continue in this way until the strap reaches the middle of the underside of the wrist. Add two or three rocailles to each thread, then take both threads through one rocaille to form a point. Knot the threads securely, as close to the beads as possible. Place a calotte (see page 13) over the knot and use pliers to press its two sides together, concealing the knot inside. Again using the pliers, attach one side of a bracelet clasp (see page 8) to the calotte and secure. Work the other side of the watch strap in the same way.

A ladder of bugle

beads and gold

rocailles makes a

really glamorous

watch strap.

Crystal, pearl and diamanté beads embroidered in simple patterns add a dash of sparkle to dramatic black accessories, making them perfect for special occasions and glamorous evenings out.

The stitched design on the drawstring purse below was the basis for the bead work (opposite).

STARRY NIGHTS

Bead work has been used for decoration since the time of the ancient Egyptians, and you will find plenty of inspiration for patterns and designs by looking through books on the history of fashion or embroidery, and by visiting museums.

The velvet purse on the left was given a nostalgic feel with beads worked in a pattern and colours reminiscent of the Art-Deco period (opposite). It could also have been given a more ornate Victorian-style decoration. Achieve an authentic look by working with fabrics and beads in designs similar to the original, or use the basic idea to create a totally new, contemporary look.

To work your own design, draw out the pattern on paper first and transfer it to the wrong side of the velvet with tailor's chalk. You can sew on the beads individually or couch them in place (see pages 10–11).

Look out for pieces of antique bead embroidery at fairs, sales and in second-hand clothes shops. These can easily be renovated and made to look as good as new, or used for totally different projects. The beautiful choker shown above was originally a shoulder strap on an evening dress. The beadwork was repaired by replacing the missing beads, and a heart-shaped drop was added to the centre of one edge. Ribbons were then sewn to either end to complete the choker.

The shoulder strap of an old evening dress provided the bead work for a glittering choker (above); and an old velvet purse becomes a fine accessory with the addition of some bead embroidery (right).

27

JET SET

Beads made from real jet are expensive, but such good glass and plastic imitations are available that you can make dramatic jewellery at an affordable price.

Imitation-jet beads

make a simple but

eye-catching

necklace.

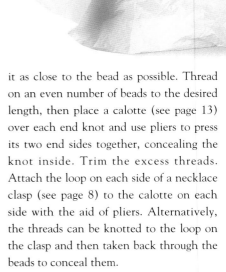

String beads on to strands of black silk thread to make necklaces, and give them an authentic Victorian look by knotting the thread between each bead. The knots must be large enough not to slip through the bead holes, so add more strands of thread if necessary.

For a necklace with a fun tassel, first make up the basic necklace. Cut several strands of thread to the desired length, plus at least half as much again to allow for the knots. Make a practice knot to check that it will be large enough. (See page 10 for advice on making knots.)

Start the necklace with a knot, then string on a bead and make the next knot, keeping it as close to the bead as possible. Thread on an even number of beads to the desired length, then place a calotte (see page 13) over each end knot and use pliers to press its two end sides together, concealing the knot inside. Trim the excess threads. Attach the loop on each side of a necklace clasp (see page 8) to the calotte on each side with the aid of pliers. Alternatively, the threads can be knotted to the loop on the clasp and then taken back through the beads to conceal them.

To make the tassel, thread small beads on to as many strands of thread as you wish. For each strand, take one end of a thread through a rocaille to act as a stop-

Beads (left) graded

in size suit this

slightly longer

necklace.

per, then take
both ends of the
thread through each
further bead. When you have
the required number of strands,
take all the thread ends through a
large bead and secure with a knot.
Knot the tassel between two beads at
the centre front of the necklace, and
take the thread ends back through the
large bead to conceal them.

A beaded tassel and

a double string of

beads make a more

ornate accessory.

BEDAZZLING BAG

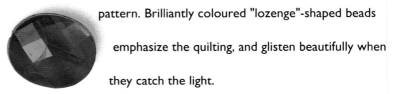

The quilted design on the bag shown here provided the inspiration for the geometric pattern. Brilliantly coloured "lozenge"-shaped beads emphasize the quilting, and glisten beautifully when they catch the light.

The slightly flattened shape of these beads lends itself to this type of decoration, as they will not catch on other objects. Large, rounder beads would create more of a problem, although small beads would look effective and could be used in greater quantities, perhaps following all the stitching lines to highlight the complete pattern.

Fabric bags are ideal for decorating in this way, as it is easy to stitch the beads in place. A leather bag is more difficult to work, but if you use a fine leather needle with its specially shaped point you can be

just as creative, using beads as a trim on a bag or in an overall pattern. Intricate designs can be worked out on a paper template of the bag before starting to sew.

Use a strong cotton thread, and fasten it securely on the inside of the bag where it will not be seen. Bring the needle through to the right side at the point at which the bead is to be attached, and take it through the bead and back through to the inside. Repeat this several times to secure the bead, as you would a button, and fasten off the thread on the inside.

The brightly coloured beads used to decorate this shoulder bag set off the vivid green satin beautifully.

JEWEL BRIGHT

Jewel-shaped and faceted beads on nylon thread make an elegant necklace to go with a smart evening outfit.

The vibrant colours used for these necklaces and earrings really sing, turning even the plainest outfit into a real stunner, and providing the perfect finishing touch.

You will achieve a more professional finish for these necklaces with special jewellery components called findings (see page 8). You will need a pair of tiny jeweller's pliers to join the findings to the beads, and wire-cutters if these are not included with the pliers.

For a linked-bead necklace, gather together a selection of head or eye pins and a necklace clasp. If you are using head pins, snip off the flat "head" with wire-cutters and use pliers to form a loop at one end (eye pins have a pre-formed loop). Insert a pin through a bead and trim any excess wire. Turn a loop in the other end of the pin (on the opposite side of the bead to the first loop). Push a pin through another bead and, using pliers, open the loop slightly and link it to a loop or "eye" on the previous bead. Continue linking the beads to the length required. Attach one part of the necklace clasp to each end, using the pliers to open and close the loops.

To make drop earrings, you will need a few head pins and a pair of ear wires, as

The many different types of beads

available will give you hundreds of

ideas for earrings.

well as pliers and wire-cutters. Simply thread the beads on to a head pin, and turn a loop at the top end. Add further beads if you wish by linking them to the loop at the top of the head pin, following the same method as for the neck-lace. When you are happy with the design, join the last loop to the loop at the bottom of the ear wire to complete the earring.

This

necklace of

linked beads and a

pendant looks shop-

bought but is

extremely easy to

make.

BOLD BANDS

Bead-woven jewellery has been created by various cultures for centuries. Different beads and patterns have produced a great range of styles, from the work of the Native Americans to the elegant examples created by the Victorians, but the dramatically different styles use the same basic techniques.

These examples are all worked in the hand. The rings are threaded on to fine wire, and can be simple band designs or tied into decorative knots. The necklet beads are woven to cover a cord (a plastic bangle can also be used for a bracelet). Using nylon thread in a beading needle, thread on beads to form a circle which fits the base circumference exactly. Take the thread through the beads again so that the foundation thread goes around the base twice, then fasten it to the beginning of the thread. For each succeeding row, add beads one at a time, taking the thread from each new bead back through the next bead on the previous row.

If you need to join a new thread, take the end of the old thread back through the work, bringing it out between two beads. Start the new thread here, bringing it out where the beading is to continue. Tie the two ends together and trim them. When the thread is pulled tight, the knot should disappear between two beads. To finish off, take the thread back through several beads and under a firm crossing thread, then secure it with a knot.

There are many methods of bead weaving, and the floral bracelet illustrates how colours can be worked in clusters. The technique for this type of weaving is shown on page 13.

Bead weaving is a quick way of creating intricately patterned jewellery in stunning colour combinations. Bright primary colours work well, as this necklet, bracelet and two simple rings demonstrate.

BELTING

Brighten up worn belts or put your own mark on a new

buy with creative bead trims. The belts on the opposite

page show how versatile bead decoration can be if you

choose the beads carefully to suit the

style of the belt.

UP

The beads on
the elastic belt
(near right) were
positioned so as
not to interfere
with the "stretch" factor,
and then stitched in place
individually. Shell, bone and antiqued gold
beads would look equally attractive,
and could make a decorative feature on

the fastening as well.

Depending on the design, the beads
can be sewn on individually, in small
groups to form a motif, or in strings which
are couched in place (see page 11). Strings
would look effective stitched to each edge
of a belt, as would two intertwined strings
sewn along the middle.

For the tartan-silk cummerbund,
first pleat a length of fabric to a
width of 5-8 cm (2-3in). Fuse
interfacing to the back to stiffen
the fabric and hold the pleats,
then turn in the raw ends and
slipstitch. Take a 3 cm (1¼ in)
wide piece of the same fabric, long
enough to fit round your waist and tie
at the back. With right sides together,
stitch down the length of this fabric, turn
it the right way out, slipstitch the raw ends
and machine stitch it in place along
the centre of the cummerbund, leaving

trailing ends for the ties.

To make the roundels, cut a pair of felt
circles for each roundel, and embroider
your chosen beads on to one circle from
each pair. Sequins, rocailles and faceted
heart-shaped beads
were used here, but
you could obviously
use any shapes or
colours of beads to
suit your fabric.
Place the second
felt circles on the
backs of the first,
and blanket stitch
the edges. Hand sew
the completed roundels
to the cummerbund, and
add further decoration,
such as the heart bead and
hanging strands in this example,
if you wish.

The beads on the black-silk
cummerbund (far right) are flat
with a central hole. In order to get
them to lie correctly, the needle was
taken through to the right side of the
belt, through the bead hole, through a
small glass rocaille bead and then back
through the central hole to the wrong side
and fastened off. These beads look effective
scattered at random, but could also work
clustered to form stylized flowers.

(From left to right) Carved wooden beads

accentuate the natural theme of an

elasticated belt; roundels of faceted

glass beads, rocailles and sequins

make a stunning decoration on

tartan silk; and flower-

shaped crystals give a

black cummerbund

a glittery finish.

HEAD TURNERS

Beads are incredibly versatile, and can be used in any number of ways on hair combs, slides and ornaments.

Beads look wonderfully effective when used to trim almost any kind of hair accessory, whether to co-ordinate the accessory with a special outfit, or simply to transform daywear to evening wear.

With just a little imagination and an assortment of beads you can produce the most original hair accessories. Choose beads to go with the base material and, depending on whether this is "soft" or "hard", sew or glue the beads in place. Small beads are quite difficult to glue successfully, but look good sewn on to ornate braid or ribbon. Wrap the ribbon around the accessories and glue in place before sewing on the beads.

Try decorating tortoiseshell Alice bands, slides and hair combs with creamy pearl

beads or small rocailles. Padded-fabric Alice bands and slides look glamorous with rich, antiqued gold or silver beads, and diamanté roundels add a touch of sparkle for evening wear. Fabric scrunchies can be edged with small beads, and plastic canvas cut into barrette shapes and decorated with ornate bead work.

Experiment and plan your designs before securing the beads in place. This is not always easy on narrow, curved surfaces, so use double-sided adhesive tape to hold the beads temporarily. If you are sewing the beads, you may find a fine, curved needle useful for awkward angles. Choose a matching or invisible thread, or add some extra texture to the design by sewing on the beads with fine ribbon or raffia.

Alice bands and scrunchies make ideal candidates for bead decoration. (Left) A black-velvet headband teamed with gold beading makes an elegant evening accessory; (centre) sparkling purple and green beads interspersed with strings of small beads enliven a plain headband; and (below) a simple edging of gold beads transforms a scrunchy in brown velvet.

GLAMOROUS GLOVES

Simple decoration can elevate a functional accessory into something special. These gloves have been trimmed with contrasting beads to produce different effects.

Customizing is the perfect way to stamp your own personal mark on an outfit. Accessories are an ideal starting point, as they are small and can often look uninteresting. Anything from hats to belts and shoes can be made to look chic and original, and you can also be sure that your outfit will be unique!

Gloves and mittens in a dazzling array of colours can be dressed up and customized to great effect. The gloves shown here can be worn with both day and evening wear, and illustrate how simple designs can transform the unexceptional into something striking. None of the designs are elaborate or complicated, and they take little time to work.

The possibilities for decorating gloves are endless, and the results can be witty and colourful or classic and understated. Try spotting tiny beads all over dark colours to give a polka-dot effect – seed pearls look sophisticated on black, while primary colours add a touch of fun. Follow the beading techniques on pages 10–11 to achieve a professional look.

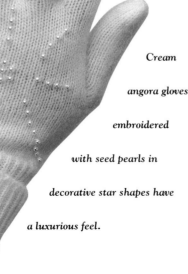

Cream angora gloves embroidered with seed pearls in decorative star shapes have a luxurious feel.

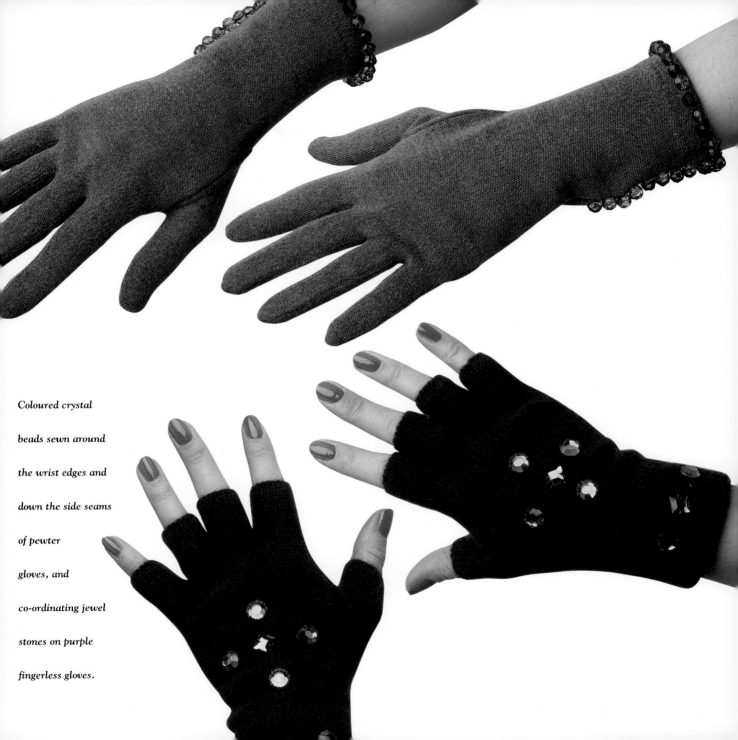

Coloured crystal beads sewn around the wrist edges and down the side seams of pewter gloves, and co-ordinating jewel stones on purple fingerless gloves.

Bring high style and glamour into your

home with unusual bead trimmings.

Tassels, fringes and "necklace" ties made from a variety

of beads can add designer detail to the

simplest of curtains.

TASSELS & TIEBACKS

Use different beads to match or contrast with your décor. Create an ethnic look by threading small wooden beads on lots of separate strands, then twisting them around each other to make an ornate braided cord. You can also use beads to make rich looped or dangling fringes to add emphasis to fabric tiebacks.

To make the tieback shown here, thread the beads on to fine wire. Fold this in half at each end and twist it together to form a firm loop. To make the tassel, thread the beads in strings on to cotton or nylon thread. Take each thread through a tiny bead to act as a stopper, then take both ends through the rest of the beads until the string is the required length.

Make as many strings as you wish, then thread all the strands through one large bead and secure them with a knot. Place a calotte (see page 13) over the knot and use pliers to press its two sides together, concealing the knot inside. Trim excess threads. Using pliers to open and close it, attach a jump ring (see page 8) to each end of the tieback and to the calotte. Link the tassel to a jump ring on the tieback. To complete, attach one part of a clasp fastening to each end of the tieback, as you would with a traditional necklace.

A simple but
sophisticated tieback
made from a
"necklace" of
glittering beads,
with a matching
tassel to add the
finishing touch.

These Victorian-style food covers with their pretty bead trims are ideal for draping over basins and jugs to keep insects at bay when dining outside on a summer's day.

CHARMING COVERS

The Victorians delighted in pretty yet practical accessories for the home, and, in the days before refrigerators, these lovely crocheted covers were an attractive and efficient way of keeping flies away from food and drink. Beads were used to decorate almost anything, and here they add a charming finishing touch while also keeping the covers in place. Dining *al fresco* is frequently spoiled by flies and other insects making a nuisance of themselves, so whether you are hosting an elegant tea party or a fun barbecue, these appealing covers are the perfect solution.

These nostalgic examples have been hand-crocheted in a fine cotton yarn to create a pretty, lacy effect. Once the main fabric has been worked, the yarn is finished off and the beads threaded on to a new piece of yarn before the edging is added, so it is easy to add beads to a bought or already completed piece of crochet.

White fabric is traditionally used, but you could of course work the covers in any colour to co-ordinate with your favourite china. You could also add beaded fringes to scraps of lace fabric or pretty fabric tablemats and coasters to complete the look and to stop them from blowing away in the breeze.

Crocheted covers edged with hanging beads make a practical and pretty feature at an outdoor meal.

MADE WITH LOVE

Impress your family and friends by sending them your love with your own individually made greetings cards. You can use beads in endless ways to create attractive designs for every possible occasion.

"Special-occasion" cards such as these have a really personal touch and are simple to make.

Inexpensive card blanks are available in every size and colour possible, and they are ideal for making your own personalized greetings cards. You could also design your own card shapes, using fine card which can be painted and decorated to create varied and interesting effects.

For original Christmas cards, cut out sequin waste in festive colours into a triangle to resemble a tree. Trim the sides to get as straight an edge as possible, and carefully glue the shape in position on the card. Glue decorative ribbon below the tree to form the pot, and put sparkling beads in the holes to look like baubles. Leave the card on a flat surface until it is completely dry and then glue it

together. You could also paint or draw festive borders with glittery marker pens to complete the effect.

Cut other shapes from sequin waste or fabric and decorate them with beads to create glittering occasion cards. For example, you can make a square look like a luxurious gift with ribbons glued to improvise the ties and beads to look like wrapping-paper details. Glue small beads straight on to cards in groups to form motifs such as hearts and stars.

Make cards to suit any occasion from birthdays to Valentines with bead embroidery. Use embroidery motifs as inspiration, and work the design on Aida (a counted-hole embroidery cloth) or similar fabric which can then be glued inside the card blank. Sew the beads in place using couching (see page 11) or half-cross stitch. You can also embroider words to suit the occasion in stranded silk or cotton embroidery thread. There are many books and magazines available with charts of alphabets and borders to give you inspiration.

Two dazzling

Christmas cards

made from shiny

sequin waste,

brilliant jewels and

decorative ribbon,

and a pretty floral

card suitable for any

type of greeting.

FLORAL FANTASY

Submerging beads in water in a clear

glass vase not only looks

striking and original, but

also conceals any

ugly flower stalks

and stems. The beads

have a practical use,

too, keeping each flower

firmly in position so that you

can produce intricate arrangements.

Be creative with your choice of beads, and select colours to tone or contrast with the flowers. Brightly coloured flowers can take strong colour combinations, while paler shades will need a softer setting. Use classic vase shapes for elegance, or modernistic styles for a strong contemporary display with designer flair.

The beads that you choose obviously need to be waterproof – plastic and glass are ideal. Some wooden beads would be unsuitable, as the insides of the holes of these beads are rarely varnished and the wood would absorb the water. You could even make your own beads from Fimo modelling clay in a marbled or mille-fiori design (see pages 14–15) to give the display of flowers a rich and exotic base.

On the left, lustrous pearls in ivory and soft pink have been used in a bowl-style vase to tone in with the pretty pastel ranunculus. The brilliant display based on hot-coloured gerberas, anemones and arum lilies (opposite, left) uses toning beads in bold shapes to create impact, while the rich purple anemones, with trailing bear grass (opposite, right), look splendid embedded in glittering, jewel-like beads.

Beads in contrasting or co-ordinating colours can create fabulous floral arrangements when displayed in plain-glass vases.

A coat of paint and the addition of sparkling crystal beads have turned the junk-shop bargain shown opposite into an elegant centrepiece that would add sophistication to any home.

An old-fashioned electric-light fitting is transformed into a superb chandelier with crystal pendants and delicate strings of beads.

CRYSTAL & CANDLELIGHT

The old electric wires and plastic "candle" bulb holders were removed from this light fitting and the metalwork cleaned in soapy water. (An electrician would be able to re-wire a lamp like this if you prefer electric light to candlelight. If you do use candles, be sure never to leave them unattended.) After being rubbed down with glasspaper to give a smooth surface and key, the fitting was sprayed with metallic pewter paint and then given an antiqued, distressed finish with boot polish. When working with spray paints, follow the manufacturer's instructions, wear a face-mask and work outside or in a well-ventilated room.

To give these candles a firm base, small metal dishes with candle spikes were glued to the bases of the old fittings and then, to complete the look, the lamp was decorated with crystal beads, which reflect the flickering candle light.

To make strings, thread small crystal beads on to invisible nylon line and secure them in place. Use triangle bails (see page 8) and fine wire to hold the crystal drops in position.

Impress your friends and spice up your dining-table with high-style salt and

pepper pots. This unusual use of beads will turn the most ordinary condiment

set into a real conversation piece!

SENSATIONAL SEASONINGS

The finished look of your salt and pepper pots can be as conservative or as wild as you choose, and worked in colours to co-ordinate with anything from your table settings to your interior décor. More elaborate effects can be achieved by covering the pots completely.

Tip some beads on to a saucer and mix the colours thoroughly. Apply a strong, waterproof, clear-drying adhesive to the pot, working on one section at a time and taking care to cover only the area to be decorated. Lay out some newspaper and, when the glue is tacky, hold the pot over the paper and sprinkle over the beads.

Leave the pot until the glue is completely dry before starting to work on another section. When the glue is dry, brush over the beads gently with your fingers to dislodge any that are loose. Add a finishing touch by gluing seed pearls randomly over the beaded sections. Wash the pots carefully by hand in tepid (but not hot) water, and allow them to dry.

Decorated with a mixture of tiny silver and

crystal rocailles and highlighted with pearls,

these basic salt and pepper pots would look

stunning in any setting.

LIGHT SHOW

A heavy fringe of crystal beads creates a look reminiscent of a bygone era on this simple glass shade.

Lampshades are one of the easiest home accessories to customize with beads, enabling you to put your own creative stamp on an interior.

The rich-looking bead fringe on the left was worked in a simple pattern using colours to co-ordinate with the shade. Two differently patterned strings were alternated all round, each being threaded on to cotton, which hangs more freely than nylon, and worked from the bottom upwards.

Cut a piece of braid or tape to fit the shade, allowing for securing and turning in raw edges. For each string, cut a length of cotton a little more than twice the required depth. Thread one end through the base bead, then both ends through the rest of the beads. Overstitch the thread to the wrong side of the braid so that the top bead sits just below the braid. To finish, wrap the braid around the bottom of the shade and stitch it securely in place. Alternatively, use double-sided adhesive tape to secure the braid on the shade.

To make the trim for the parchment shade opposite, string the beads on to

nylon thread – the finished length will need to be the circumference of the bottom edge of the shade plus at least half as much again, depending on the width and depth of the drop. To secure the string, first pierce holes at regular intervals around the bottom of the shade, through the binding, to prevent the shade from tearing. Next, fold the nylon thread double at the point the drop is to start, and push this loop through the hole to the wrong side. Overstitch the loop firmly to the binding, adding a small blob of glue to secure. Once the string is in place, glue wooden disc beads over the holes to give a neat finish.

A parchment shade enhanced with a scalloped fringe of rich wooden beads.

When a beautiful curtain of glass beads catches the light, it

casts magical kaleidoscopic patterns all around it, making a

feature of the dullest of windows. A beaded curtain can

also transform a doorway or

archway to create a really

eye-catching decoration.

WINDOW DRESSING

First choose a suitable support for your curtain. This simple curtain for a small window was strung on to dowelling and supported on cup hooks, but a heavier version would need to be screwed to the wall, or to the window or door frame. Strong nylon fishing line will take the weight of the beads. The drops at the bottom of this curtain were attached using triangle bails (see page 8), which allow the beads to hang freely, and the thread was knotted to each triangle bail.

First measure the width and drop of the window and work out the pattern on paper. Cut the support to size and, using a craft knife, score

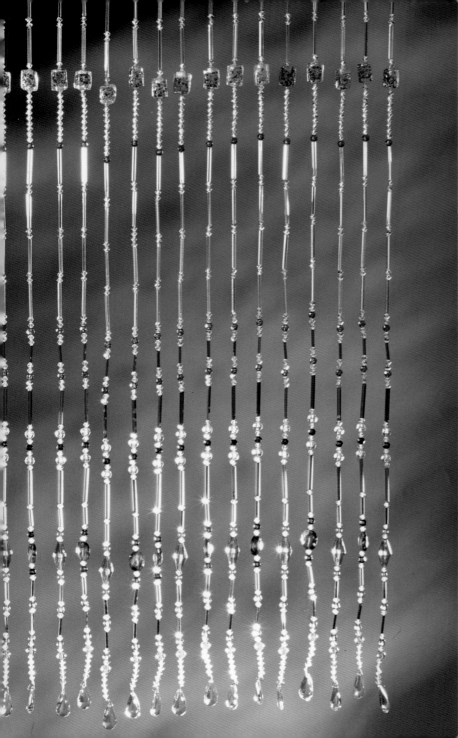

grooves along its length to hold the strings securely in position.

Cut the nylon line into the number of lengths required, adding 15 cm (6 in) to the drop to allow for knotting and threading the ends back through the beads to conceal them. Knot each strand securely to the support, leaving a 7.5 cm (3 in) "tail".

String on the beads in the desired pattern, working the "tail" at the top through the first few beads as you go to conceal it. Knot the thread as closely as possible to the final bead, and dab a blob of clear-drying glue on to the knot for extra strength. Push the tail back up through the beads to conceal it. Continue working in this way to complete all the strands.

Glass-bead curtains provide a stylish alternative to net. This design uses a mix of large and small beads in subtle blues and greens, but you could use any combination of colours.

TREE TREASURES

The beautiful bead and sequin decorations opposite are simple to make and would grace any Christmas tree.

Decking the Christmas tree with your own hand-made ornaments will create an attractive and original centre-piece. Use beads and sequins to produce traditional shapes in seasonal colours.

It is easy to turn pressed-cotton or styrofoam balls into stunning baubles using beads and sequins. Create an ornate finish by pinning sequins in rows all over the ball with classic flat-head or glass-head pins, and either trim the bauble with ribbon or make your own braid by weaving tiny rocailles together. You could produce a simpler look by trimming the plain ball with a woven bead braid, or by painting the ball itself gold, silver or any other seasonal colour first.

Bugle beads make beautiful stars. Use invisible or matching thread and begin by threading on six bugles, taking the end of the thread back through the first one. Draw up the beads into a hexagon shape. Put two further bugles on to the thread, then take the thread back through one of the bugles forming the hexagon as if making a backstitch. Take the thread all the way through the next bugle on the hexagon, then thread on two more bugles and make the backstitch. Continue all round until you have a six-pointed star. Fasten the thread ends securely, and make a hanging loop with new thread from one point.

The pretty icicles shown opposite are made using special beads, which sit neatly on top of one another to form the icicle shape. To make stars, glue five same-sized beads together in a ring. When dry, make the points by gluing smaller and smaller beads together, radiating out from the central beads.

Hand-knitted in simple stocking stitch in a standard double-knitting yarn, these delightful baubles add a dash of colour to the tree at Christmas, and are also perfect for using up oddments of wool.

FESTIVE BAUBLES

An inspired choice of yarn can produce stunning effects on these highly original Christmas decorations. A luxurious chenille in brilliant jewel colours creates a rich velvety bauble, for example. Silky ribbon yarns or glittering metallics have a lustrous sheen which adds a touch of glamour, while white mohair resembles soft fluffy snowballs, especially if brushed.

To knit the decorations, use the recommended needle size and tension quoted on the ball band (although for these fun baubles, traditional techniques can be ignored as long as you are happy with the resulting knitted fabric). For a simple stocking-stitch bauble, cast on between 11 and 15 stitches, depending on the yarn and size of ball required. Increase in every stitch on the first (knit) row to double the initial number of stitches. Knit a further 14 to 18 rows (or as desired) in stocking stitch (knit one row, purl one row), ending on a purl row.

On the next row, decrease back to the original number of stitches by knitting two together across the row. Break the yarn, leaving a long "tail", and thread this back through the remaining stitches. Slip the stitches off the needle.

Using a tapestry needle threaded with the same yarn, run a row of gathering stitches along the cast-on edge, draw it up tightly and fasten it off. Stitch the side seam, matching the row ends, and turn the fabric through to the right side. Stuff the bauble with wadding. Pull up the length of yarn at the top, gathering the stitches tightly, and fasten it off. Make a hanging loop in matching yarn or metallic thread and secure this to the top.

Decorate each bauble extravagantly with beads and sequins. You can either sew these on, or glue them in place using an appropriate craft adhesive.

Bright knitted ornaments trimmed with beads make a lovely change from shop-bought tree decorations, and sparkle beautifully under the lights.

The gentle sound of tinkling windchimes has

a wonderfully soothing effect,

reminding one of mystical, far-off

lands. Hang them in

windows or doorways to catch the slightest

breath of air.

Simple bone beads,

some carved with

exotic patterns,

along with cinnabar

and silver beads,

CHIMERICAL CHIMES

make beautiful

windchimes. Hang

them by a door or

window and enjoy

their soft sounds

as they sway in

the breeze.

The mix of subtle, neutral colours highlighted with cinnabar and silver emphasizes the design of these simple chimes. They were hung from a cheap plastic curtain ring bound with fine string to enhance the natural theme. You could steep the string in cold tea for a few hours to darken it subtly, or use raffia, twine or brightly coloured cord to bind the ring if you prefer.

For the outer ring, make up six bead strings on strong, invisible nylon line, each measuring approximately 25 cm (10 in) when completed. To do this, cut the six threads into lengths of 60 cm (24 in), fold each in half and take one end of the thread through the bell first and then both ends through the rest of the beads. Tie and knot each of these securely to the plastic ring. Bind string tightly round the ring to cover it completely, taking the string across the centre and back again to form the middle bar.

To make up the centrepiece, start with three strings. Bring these together at the top by threading all the ends together through more beads. Plait three lengths of string together to make the hanging thread, and knot this and the centrepiece to the middle bar. The finished windchimes will add a restful touch to any corner of your home.

ACKNOWLEDGMENTS

The author would like to thank the following people for their help and support while putting this book together. Firstly, Ells & Farrier, Creative Beadcraft, The Brighton Bead Shop and Janet Coles for kindly supplying all the fabulous beads used to create the projects; Liz Gill, Lesley Stanfield, Jane Moody, Elise Mann, and Lindsey Stock for their much-appreciated help with the designs; and last, but not least, my family, especially my mother and sister Lisa, without whom the book would not have been completed.

Quarto would like to thank the following bead suppliers:
Brighton Bead Shop, 21 Sydney Street, Brighton, Sussex BN1 4EN
Creative Beadcraft, Denmark Works, Sheepcote Dell Road, Beamond End, Nr.
Amersham, Bucks HP7 ORX
Ells & Farrier, 20 Beak Street, London W1
Janet Coles, Perdiswell Cottage, Bilford Road, Worcester WR3 8QA

Quarto would also like to thank the craftspeople who supplied projects for the book:
Janet Coles 32-3; Liz Gill 26-7, 37 (centre); Elise Mann 38-9, 58-9; Jane Moody 60-1;
Lesley Stanfield 44-5. All other projects were done by Jo Moody.

The flowers on pages 48-9 were supplied by Paula Pryke.